This is a recorder.

AF146439

The recorder is a woodwind instrument.

woodwind

wood

plastic

It can be
wooden or plastic.

holes
/hoʊlz/

7
6
5
4
3
2
1

fingers

It has seven finger holes...

...and a thumb hole at the back.

thumb

A recorder has three parts:

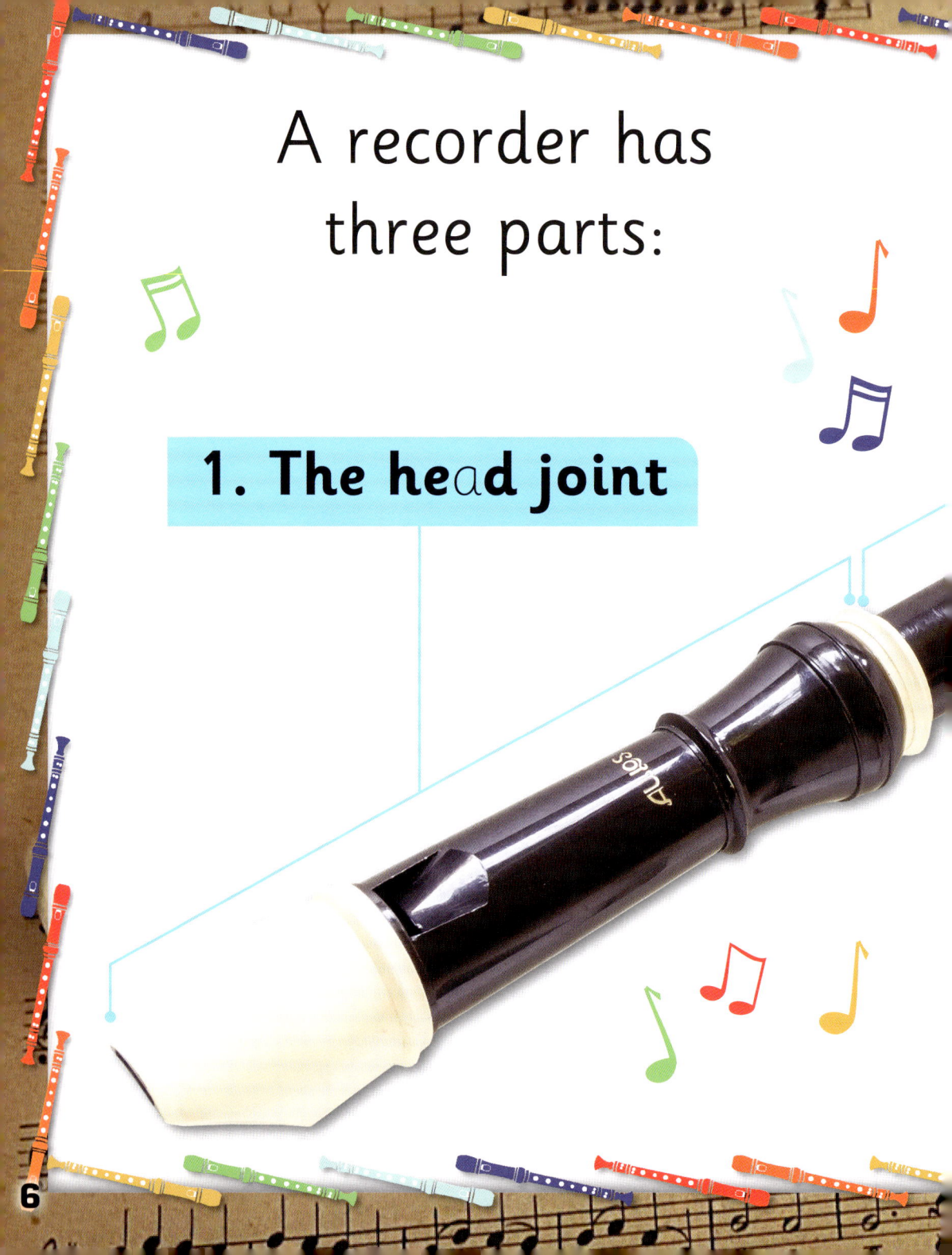

1. The head joint

2. The middle

3. The foot joint

The recorder is fun, too!